1.

Penguin Education
Junior Voices The fourth book
edited by Geoffrey Summerfield

Junior Voices The fourth book

edited by Geoffrey Summerfield

掌中浪

With 37 illustrations, 14 in colour

Penguin Books

Penguin Books Ltd, Harmondsworth,
Middlesex, England
Penguin Books Australia Ltd, Ringwood,
Victoria, Australia

First published 1970
This selection copyright © Geoffrey Summerfield, 1970

Filmset in Great Britain by
Butler & Tanner Ltd, Frome and London
Colour reproduction by Newgate Press Ltd,
London
Made and printed by W. S. Cowell Ltd,
at the Butter Market, Ipswich

Contents

Knock Knock, Who's There?

Chester. Chester who? Chester song at twilight.
Cecil. Cecil who? Cecil have music wherever she goes.
Hoffman. Hoffman who? I'll hoffman I'll puff an' I'll
blow yer house in.
Argo. Argo who? Argo chase yerself.
Morris. Morris who? Morris Saturday – next day's Sunday.
Marcella. Marcella who? Marcella's fulla water.
Major. Major who? Major answer the door didn't I?
Thermos. Thermos who? Thermos be someone waiting
who feels the way I do.
Arthur. Arthur who? Arthur any more at home like you?
Agatha. Agatha who? Agatha feeling you're foolin'.
Akron. Akron who? Akron give you anything but love, baby.
Alby. Alby who? Alby glad when today's over.
Hassan. Hassan who? Hassan a body here seen Kelly?
Irving. Irving who? Irving a good time, wish you were here.
Cigarette. Cigarette who? Cigarette life if you don't weaken.
Bob. Bob who? Bob ba black sheep, have you any wool?
Fletcher. Fletcher who? Relax and fletcher self go.
Wendy. Wendy who? Wendy moon comes over the
mountain.
Caesar. Caesar who? Caesar jolly good fellow, caesar jolly
good fellow.
Thistle. Thistle who? Thistle be a lesson to me.

BOB DUNN

The Door

Go and open the door.
  Maybe outside there's
  a tree, or a wood,
  a garden,
  or a magic city.

Go and open the door.
  Maybe a dog's rummaging.
  Maybe you'll see a face,
or an eye,
or the picture
                of a picture.

Go and open the door.
  If there's a fog
  it will clear.

Go and open the door.
  Even if there's only
  the darkness ticking,
  even if there's only
  the hollow wind,
  even if
        nothing
                is there,
  go and open the door.

At least
there'll be
a draught.

MIROSLAV HOLUB Czechoslovakian poem translated by Ian Milner

An Ordinary Day

I took my mind a walk
Or my mind took me a walk –
Whichever was the truth of it.

The light glittered on the water
Or the water glittered in the light.
Cormorants stood on a tidal rock

With their wings spread out,
Stopping no traffic. Various ducks
Shilly-shallied here and there

On the shilly-shallying water.
An occasional gull yelped. Small flowers
Were doing their level best

To bring to their kerb bees like
Aerial charabancs. Long weeds in the clear
Water did Eastern dances, unregarded

By shoals of darning needles. A cow
Started a moo but thought
Better of it . . . And my feet took me home

And my mind observed to me,
Or I to it, how ordinary
Extraordinary things are or

How extraordinary ordinary
Things are, like the nature of the mind
And the process of observing.

NORMAN MacCAIG

Morning Worship

I wake and hear it raining.
Were I dead, what would I give
Lazily to lie here,
Like this, and live?

Or better yet: birdsong,
Brightening and spreading –
How far would I come then
To be at the world's wedding?

Now that I lie, though,
Listening, living,
(Oh, but not forever,
Oh, end arriving)

How shall I praise them:
All the sweet beings
Eternally that outlive
Me and my dying?

Mountains, I mean; wind, water, air;
Grass, and huge trees; clouds, flowers,
And thunder, and night.

Turtles, I mean, and toads; hawks, herons, owls;
Graveyards, and towns, and trout; roads, gardens,
Red berries, and deer.

Lightning, I mean, and eagles; fences; snow;
Sunrise, and ferns; waterfalls, serpents,
Green islands, and sleep.

Horses, I mean; butterflies, whales;
Mosses, and stars; and gravelly
Rivers, and fruit.

Oceans, I mean; black valleys; corn;
Brambles, and cliffs; rock, dirt, dust, ice;
And warnings of flood.

How shall I name them?
And in what order?
Each would be first.
Omission is murder.

Maidens, I mean, and apples; needles; leaves;
Worms, and planets, and clover; whirlwinds; dew;
Bulls; geese –

Stop. Lie still.
You will never be done . . .

MARK VAN DOREN

Interruption to a Journey

The hare we had run over
Bounced about the road
On the springing curve
Of its spine.

Cornfields breathed in the darkness.
We were going through the darkness and
The breathing cornfields from one
Important place to another.

We broke the hare's neck
And made that place, for a moment,
The most important place there was,
Where a bowstring was cut
And a bow broken for ever
That had shot itself through so many
Darknesses and cornfields.

It was left in that landscape.
It left us in another.

NORMAN MacCAIG

The Names of the Months

Jaguary
Cassowary
Marten
Mandrill
Maybird
Coon
Shoofly
Locust
Serpent bear
Octopus
North Pole bear
Remem bear

CHRISTIAN MORGENSTERN German poem translated by Max Knight

The Wild Geese Leave

Wild geese! I know
   that they did eat the barley;
      yet, when they go . . .

YASUI Japanese poem translated by Harold G. Henderson

Haiku

Had they no voice
   the herons would be lost –
      this morning's snow!

CHIYO Japanese poem translated by Harold G. Henderson

stretched out

stretched out
on the grass
minding my business –
this bird, splat!
right on my head

ISHIKAWA TAKUBOKU Japanese poem translated by Carl Sesar

Beauty

The usually hateful crow:
   he, too – this morning,
      on the snow!

MATSUO BASHŌ Japanese poem translated by Harold G. Henderson

The Starlings in George Square

1   Sundown on the high stonefields!
The darkening roofscape stirs –
thick – alive with starlings
gathered singing in the square –
like a shower of arrows they cross
the flash of a western window,
they bead the wires with jet,
they nestle preening by the lamps
and shine, sidling by the lamps
and sing, shining, they stir
the homeward hurrying crowds.
A man looks up and points
smiling to his son beside him
wide-eyed at the clamour on those cliffs –
it sinks, shrills out in waves,
levels to a happy murmur,
scatters in swooping arcs,
a stab of confused sweetness
that pierces the boy like a story,
a story more than a song.
He will never forget that evening,
the silhouette of the roofs,
the starlings by the lamps.

2   The City Chambers are hopping mad.
Councillors with rubber plugs in their ears!
Secretaries closing windows!
Window-cleaners want protection and danger money.
The Lord Provost can't hear herself think, man.
What's that?
Lord Provost, can't hear herself think.

At the General Post Office
the clerks write Three Pounds Starling in the savings-books.
Each telephone-booth is like an aviary.
I tried to send a parcel to County Kerry but –
The cables to Cairo got fankled, sir.
What's that?
I said the cables to Cairo got fankled.

And as for the City Information Bureau –
I'm sorry I can't quite chirrup did you twit –
No I wanted to twee but perhaps you can't cheep –
Would you try once again, that's better, I – sweet –
When's the last boat to Milngavie? Tweet?
What's that?
I said when's the last boat to Milngavie?

3   There is nothing for it now but scaffolding:
     clamp it together, send for the bird-men,
     Scarecrow Strip for the window-ledge landings.
     Cameron's Repellent on the overhead wires.
     Armour our pediments against eavesdroppers.
     This is a human outpost. Save our statues.
     Send back the jungle. And think of the joke:
     as it says in the papers, It is very comical
     to watch them alight on the plastic rollers
     and take a tumble. So it doesn't kill them?
     All right, so who's complaining? This isn't Peking
     where they shoot the sparrows for hygiene and cash.
     So we're all humanitarians, locked in our cliff-dwellings
     encased in our repellent, guano-free and guilt-free.
     The Lord Provost sings in her marble hacienda.
     The Postmaster-General licks an audible stamp.
     Sir Walter is vexed that his column's deserted.
     I wonder if we really deserve starlings?
     There is something to be said for these joyous messengers
     that we repel in our indignant orderliness.
     They lift up the eyes, they lighten the heart,
     and some day we'll decipher that sweet frenzied whistling
     as they wheel and settle along our hard roofs
     and take those grey buttresses for home.
     One thing we know they say, after their fashion.
     They like the warm cliffs of man.

EDWIN MORGAN

dog in the street

dog in the street
stretching
in a nice long yawn –
pure envy
I do likewise

ISHIKAWA TAKUBOKU Japanese poem translated by Carl Sesar

King of Beasts

To come close to a city
Is a hard matter
For one man – all these hawks
And crocodiles, milch-cows and
Pretty posies, sting-nettles and basking
Sharks wear human faces. Easy
For a man-fox to recognize
A man-fox or a blue hare being
A man; but how is he to know
A disguised shrimp or a nightingale
With a pipe in its mouth?

              – The only one
There's no mistake about is
The indifferent lion lolling
Through the jungle in the back of
His Rolls-Royce. When you see him,
Keep off the Zebra crossing – dive
Down an alley, if you're a rabbit,
Or sing, if you're a lark,
Straight up in the air.

NORMAN MacCAIG

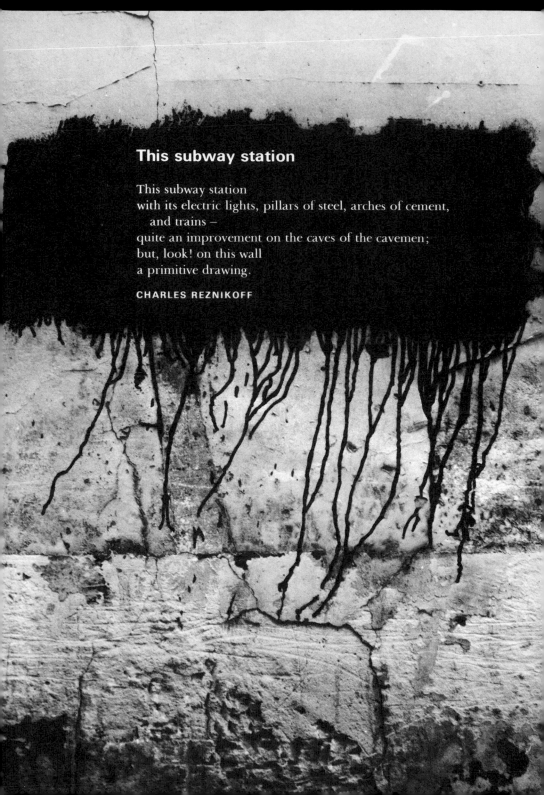

This subway station

This subway station
with its electric lights, pillars of steel, arches of cement,
   and trains —
quite an improvement on the caves of the cavemen;
but, look! on this wall
a primitive drawing.

CHARLES REZNIKOFF

The Meadow Mouse

1   In a shoe box stuffed in an old nylon stocking
Sleeps the baby mouse I found in the meadow,
Where he trembled and shook beneath a stick
Till I caught him up by the tail and brought him in,
Cradled in my hand,
A little quaker, the whole body of him trembling,
His absurd whiskers sticking out like a cartoon-mouse,
His feet like small leaves,
Little lizard-feet,
Whitish and spread wide when he tried to struggle away,
Wriggling like a miniscule puppy.

Now he's eaten his three kinds of cheese and drunk from
    his bottle-cap watering-trough –
So much he just lies in one corner,
His tail curled under him, his belly big
As his head; his bat-like ears
Twitching, tilting toward the least sound.

Do I imagine he no longer trembles
When I come close to him?
He seems no longer to tremble.

2   But this morning the shoe-box house on the back porch
    is empty.
Where has he gone, my meadow mouse,
My thumb of a child that nuzzled in my palm? –
To run under the hawk's wing,
Under the eye of the great owl watching from the elm-tree,
To live by courtesy of the shrike, the snake, the tom-cat.

I think of the nestling fallen into the deep grass,
The turtle gasping in the dusty rubble of the highway,
The paralytic stunned in the tub, and the water rising, –
All things innocent, hapless, forsaken.

THEODORE ROETHKE

A Dog in the Quarry

The day was so bright
    that even birdcages flew open.
The breasts of lawns
    heaved with joy
and the cars on the highway
    sang the great song of asphalt.
At Lobzy a dog fell in the quarry
    and howled.
Mothers pushed their prams out of the park opposite
because babies cannot sleep
    when a dog howls,
and a fat old pensioner was cursing the Municipality:
they let the dog fall in the quarry and then leave him
        there,
and this, if you please, has been going on since morning.

Towards evening even the trees
    stopped blossoming
and the water at the bottom of the quarry
    grew green with death.
But still the dog howled.

Then along came some boys
and made a raft out of two logs
and two planks.
And a man left on the bank
a briefcase . . .
he laid aside his briefcase
and sailed with them.

Their way led across a green puddle
to the island where the dog waited.
It was a voyage like
    the discovery of America,
a voyage like
    the quest of Theseus.
The dog fell silent,
    the boys stood like statues
and one of them punted with a stick,
the waves shimmered nervously,

tadpoles swiftly
   flickered out of the wake,
the heavens
   stood still,
and the man stretched out his hand.

It was a hand
   reaching out across the ages,
it was a hand
   linking
   one world with another,
   life with death,
it was a hand
   joining everything together,
it caught the dog by the scruff of its neck

and then they sailed back
to the music of
an immense fanfare
of the dog's yapping . . .

MIROSLAV HOLUB
Czechoslovakian poem translated by George Theiner

A Yellow Circle

A green
string
is fastened
to the earth
at its apex
a yellow
circle
of silky
superimposed
spokes.
The sun
is its mother.

halo
quickly fading

Later,
the string
is taller.
The circle
is white –
an aureole
of evanescent
hairs
the wind
makes breathe

Later still
it is altered;
the green
string
is thicker,
the white
circle
bald
on one side.
It is a half
circle
the wind lifts away.

MAY SWENSON

Four Natural Songs (Riddles)

1 Awoke and stretched in all the bodies
   lofted on sinewy air   Clipped out
   beak-shaped cries and skinned the mist
   from the morning

2 Humped up sucked in all my thongs
   belly-deep to the roaring core   Recoiled
   for a big yellow bloom   Burst and hurled
   wide open pods of light everywhere

3 Pricked up out of each pore urgent ambitious
   itching to be even   Scurried and spread
   so all is kept level   Forever unfinished
   my mass fernal mystery   Ants read its roots
   tell its juices to sand

4 Loosened and looled elongate in hammocks
   of blue   Evasive of shape and the eggshell's
   curve   Without taint or tint or substance
   dissolved in fleecy sloth

MAY SWENSON

Clouds

Clouds come from time to time –
   and bring to men a chance to rest
      from looking at the moon.

MATSUO BASHŌ Japanese poem translated by Harold G. Henderson

On the Quay

What they say on the quay is,
  'There's no shelter
From the blow of the wind,
  Or the sea's banter, –
There's two more to drown
  The week after.'

THEODORE ROETHKE

The Wreckers' Prayer

Give us a wrack or two, Good Lard,
For winter in Tops'il Tickle be hard,
Wid grey frost creepin' like mortal sin
And perishin' lack of bread in the bin.

A grand rich wrack, us do humbly pray,
Busted abroad at the break o'day
An' hove clear in 'crost Tops'il Reef,
Wid victuals an' gear to beguile our grief.

God of reefs an' tides an' sky,
Heed ye our need and hark to our cry!
Bread by the bag an' beef by the cask –
Ease for sore bellies bes all we ask.

One grand wrack – or maybe two? –
Wid gear an' victuals to see us through
'Til Spring starts up like the leap of day
An' the fish strike back into Tops'il Bay.

One rich wrack – for Thy hand bes strong!
A barque or a brig from up-along
Bemused by thy twisty tides, O Lard!
For winter in Tops'il Tickle bes hard.

Loud an' long will us sing yer praise.
Merciful Fadder, O Ancient of Days,
Master of fog, an' tide, an' reef!
Heave us a wrack to beguile our grief. Amen.

THEODORE GOODRIDGE ROBERTS

Eh?

He was so short that to mount his horse he had to stand on his head to get his foot in the stirrup.

TRADITIONAL AUSTRALIAN

Larrikin Language

Tough

'Tis the everyday Australian
   Has a language of his own,
Has a language, or a slanguage,
   Which can simply stand alone.
And a 'dickin pitch to kid us'
   Is a synonym for 'lie',
And to 'nark it' means to stop it,
   And to 'nit it' means to fly!

And his naming of the coinage
   Is a mystery to some,
With his 'quid' and 'half-a-caser'
   And his 'deener' and his 'scrum'.
And a 'tin-back' is a party
   Who's remarkable for luck,
And his food is called his 'tucker'
   Or his 'panem' or his 'chuck'.

A policeman is a 'johnny'
   Or a 'copman' or a 'trap',
And a thing obtained on credit
   Is invariably 'strap'.
A conviction's known as 'trouble',
   And a gaol is called a 'jug',
And a sharper is a 'spieler'   swindler
   And a simpleton's a 'tug'.

If he hits a man in fighting
    That is what he calls a 'plug',
If he borrows money from you
    He will say he 'bit your lug'.
And to 'shake it' is to steal it,
    And to 'strike it' is to beg;
And a jest is 'poking borak',
    And a jester 'pulls your leg'.

Things are 'cronk' when they go wrongly
    In the language of the 'push',
But when things go as he wants 'em
    He declares it is 'all cush'.
When he's bright he's got a 'napper',
    And he's 'ratty' when he's daft,
And when looking for employment
    He is 'out o'blooming graft'.

And his clothes he calls his 'clobber'
    Or his 'togs', but what of that
When a 'castor' or a 'kady'
    Is the name he gives his hat!
And our undiluted English
    Is a fad to which we cling,
But the great Australian slanguage
    Is a truly awful thing!

W.T. GOODGE

Odds and Ends

A BLUNDER OF BOYS
A GIGGLE OF GIRLS
A CONSTERNATION OF MOTHERS
A GRUMBLING OF BUSES

A HUMBUG OF PACKAGES
A GUNDULUM OF GARBAGE CANS

A SCRIBBITCH OF PAPERS
A TUMBLETELL OF CHURCH BELLS

A SNIGGLEMENT OF STRING
A TRIBULATION OF CHILDREN

ALASTAIR REID

The Hob-Nailed Boots what Farver Wore

My farver's feet filled up arf a street
So his boots was in proportion,
And the kids he'd squash in a week, by gosh!
It really was a caution.
Well, me and me bruvvers at the age of four,
All wrapped up cosy in a box of straw,
Till eleven in the morning used to sleep and snore,
In the hob-nailed boots what farver wore.

When Madge and Flo went to Southend, so
As money they'd be saving
Father's boots were seen as a bathin' machine
Where the bathers 'ud change for bathin'.
Well, while they was changin', they forgot, I'm sure,
The hole he had cut for his corns, and cor!
The boys started giggling at what they saw –
In the hob-nailed boots what farver wore.

Now, we had a goat with a cast iron throat,
Though she never used to bite us;
She died one Sunday in the afternoon
Of acute appendicitis.
Now, she had whiskers used to touch the floor
And when they was plaited by the kids next door
They made the finest laces that you ever saw
For the hob-nailed boots what farver wore.

When I went to school, well, I felt a fool,
For one day when we was drillin',
The teacher said, 'Toe the line fathead',
And I did that most unwillin'.
She said, 'I'll-tell-you-and-I've-told-you-before,
Don't keep backin' through the schoolhouse door.'
'Well, just toe the line!' said the kids with a roar,
'In the hob-nail boots what farver wore.'

On the Lord Mayor's day just to shout hoorah,
Father went and how he sauced 'em;
But his plates of meat stuck across the street
So the Lord Mayor drove across them.
As he was going through the Guildhall door
Father fell flat across his back and swore,
And the crowd started booing then, 'cos all they saw
Was the hob-nailed boots what farver wore.

TRADITIONAL ENGLISH

The barber shop

The barber shop has curtains
but it must have been a long time since they were washed
for they are a dark grey
and falling apart;
the window itself is dirty
and whatever signs it has are grey with dust.
The barber stands in the doorway
wearing a coat of uncertain white
over dirty trousers –
and he needs a shave badly.
The shop is called in bold letters
'Sanitary Barber Shop',
and there are those, I suppose, who believe it.

CHARLES REZNIKOFF

The man put green spectacles on his cow

'The man put green spectacles on his cow and fed her
sawdust.
Maybe she would believe it was grass.
But she didn't. She died on him.'

CARL SANDBURG

Tall Stories

A farmer, tired of dry farming in desert country, decided to
move house to a place of eternal rain. When he was asked
why, he said, 'I'm tired of sweating dust, that's why. Out here
the only rains are dust storms. Buzzards have to wear goggles
and fly backwards to keep from choking to death, and grass-
hoppers carry haversacks to keep from starving. The only
fish to be caught in dry lakes are dried herring, and my mouth
is always so dry that the only way I can whistle to my dog
is by ringing a bell.'

A traveller from a wet region where the rain was almost
continuous decided to move house. He explained, 'This place
is too wet for me. The only time the sun ever shines is when
it rains. Even the pores of my skin are sprouting watercress.
I could stand it when water-bugs took the place of flies, and
when the chickens grew webbed feet and their eggs hatched
out turtles; I just laughed at the bull-frogs croaking on the
head of my bed and when my wife got water on the knee. But
when I started catching cat-fish in the sitting room mouse-
trap I reckoned it was time to move.'

ANONYMOUS AMERICAN

The Death of Ned Kelly

Ned Kelly fought the rich men in country and in town,
Ned Kelly fought the troopers until they ran him down;
He thought that he had fooled them, for he was hard to find,
But he rode into Glenrowan with the troopers close behind.

chief trooper 'Come out of that, Ned Kelly,' the head zarucker calls,
'Come out and leave your shelter, or we'll shoot it full of holes.'
'If you take *me*,' says Kelly, 'that's not the speech to use;
I've lived to spite your order, I'll die the way I choose!'

'Come out of that, Ned Kelly, you done a lawless thing:
You robbed and fought the squatters, Ned Kelly, you must
    swing.'
'If those who rob,' says Kelly, 'are all condemned to die,
You had better hang the squatters; they've stolen more than I.'

'You'd best come out, Ned Kelly, you done the government
    wrong,
For you held up the coaches that bring the gold along.'
'Go tell your boss,' says Kelly, 'who lets the rich go free,
That your bloody rich men's government will never govern me.'

'You talk all right, Ned Kelly, your tongue is slick, I own;
But I have men to help me and you are all alone.'
They burned the roof above him, they fired the walls about,
And head to foot in armour Ned Kelly stumbled out.

Although his guns were empty he took them by surprise;
He wore an iron breastplate and armour on his thighs.
Although his guns were empty he made them turn and flee,
But one came in behind him and shot him in the knee.

And so they took Ned Kelly and hanged him in the jail,
For he fought single-handed although in iron mail.
And no man single-handed can hope to break the bars;
It's a thousand like Ned Kelly who'll hoist the Flag of Stars.

JOHN MANIFOLD

Go Down, Moses

Go down, Moses,
Way down in Egypt land,
Tell old Pharaoh
To let my people go.

When Israel was in Egypt land,
Let my people go,
Oppressed so hard they could not stand,
Let my people go.

Go down, Moses,
Way down in Egypt land,
Tell old Pharaoh,
'Let my people go.'

'Thus saith the Lord,' bold Moses said,
'Let my people go;
If not I'll smite your first-born dead
Let my people go.'

Go down, Moses,
Way down in Egypt land,
Tell old Pharoah,
'Let my people go!'

TRADITIONAL AMERICAN

A Pict Song

Rome never looks where she treads.
    Always her heavy hooves fall
On our stomachs, our hearts or our heads;
    And Rome never heeds when we bawl.
Her sentries pass on – that is all,
    And we gather behind them in hordes,
And plot to reconquer the Wall,
    With only our tongues for our swords.

We are the Little Folk – we!
   Too little to love or to hate.
Leave us alone and you'll see
   How we can drag down the State!
We are the worm in the wood!
   We are the rot at the root!
We are the taint in the blood!
   We are the thorn in the foot!

Mistletoe killing an oak –
   Rats gnawing cables in two –
Moths making holes in a cloak –
   How they must love what they do!
Yes – and we Little Folk too,
   We are busy as they –
Working our works out of view –
   Watch, and you'll see it some day!

No indeed! We are not strong,
   But we know Peoples that are.
Yes, and we'll guide them along
   To smash and destroy you in War!
We shall be slaves just the same?
   Yes, we have always been slaves,
But you – you will die of the shame,
   And then we shall dance on your graves!

We are the little Folk – we!
   Too little to love or to hate.
Leave us alone and you'll see
   How we can drag down the State!
We are the worm in the wood!
   We are the rot at the root!
We are the taint in the blood!
   We are the thorn in the foot!

RUDYARD KIPLING

Roman Wall Blues

Over the heather the wet wind blows,
I've lice in my tunic and a cold in my nose.

The rain comes pattering out of the sky,
I'm a Wall soldier, I don't know why.

The mist creeps over the hard grey stone,
My girl's in Tungria; I sleep alone.

Aulus goes hanging around her place,
I don't like his manners, I don't like his face.

Piso's a Christian, he worships a fish;
There'd be no kissing if he had his wish.

She gave me a ring but I diced it away;
I want my girl and I want my pay.

When I'm a veteran with only one eye
I shall do nothing but look at the sky.

W.H. AUDEN

Pretty Boy Floyd

Come and gather 'round me, children,
A story I will tell
About Pretty Boy Floyd, the outlaw,
Oklahoma knew him well.

It was in the town of Shawnee
On a Saturday afternoon,
His wife beside him in the wagon,
As into town they rode.

There a deputy sheriff approached him
In a manner rather rude,
Using vulgar words of anger,
And his wife, she overheard.

Pretty Boy grabbed a log chain,
The deputy grabbed his gun,
And in the fight that followed
He laid that deputy down.

Then he took to the trees and timber
To live a life of shame,
Every crime in Oklahoma
Was added to his name.

Yes, he took to the river bottom
Along the river shore,
And Pretty Boy found a welcome
At every farmer's door.

The papers said that Pretty Boy
Had robbed a bank each day,
While he was setting in some farmhouse,
Three hundred miles away.

There's many a starving farmer
The same old story told,
How the outlaw paid their mortgage
And saved their little home.

Others tell you 'bout a stranger
That come to beg a meal,
And underneath his napkin
Left a thousand-dollar bill.

It was in Oklahoma City,
It was on a Christmas Day,
There came a whole carload of groceries
With a note to say:

'You say that I'm an outlaw,
You say that I'm a thief,
Here's a Christmas dinner
For the families on relief.'

Yes, as through this world I've rambled
I've seen lots of funny men,
Some will rob you with a six gun,
And some with a fountain pen.

But as through your life you'll travel,
Wherever you may roam,
You won't never see no outlaw
Drive a family from their home.

WOODIE GUTHRIE

unforgettable

unforgettable
that face –
man in the street
laughing, police
dragging him off

ISHIKAWA TAKUBOKU Japanese poem translated by Carl Sesar

Whisky in the Jar

As I was going over Gilgarra Mountain,
I met Colonel Pepper and his money he was counting.
I drew forth my pistols and I rattled my sabre
Saying 'Stand and deliver, for I am a bold deceiver.'

>Musha ringum duram da,
>Whack! fol de daddy-o,
>Whack! fol de daddy-o,
>There's whisky in the jar.

The shining golden coins did sure look bright and jolly,
I took the money home and I gave it to my Molly,
She promised and she vowed that she never would deceive me,
But the Divil's in the women and they never can be easy.

Now when I awakened between the hours of six and seven,
Guards were standing round me in numbers odd and even,
I flew to my pistols, but, alas, I was mistaken,
For I fired off my pistols and a prisoner was taken.

They put me in jail without judge or writing,
For robbing Colonel Pepper on Gilgarra Mountain,
But they didn't take my fists, so I knocked down the sentry
And I bid a long farewell to the Judge in Sligo town.

TRADITIONAL IRISH

Jive Talk

Beat up your chops	talk a lot
Benders	knees
Benny or bear	overcoat
Chimer	alarm clock
Chinch	bedbug
Collar all jive	understand everything
Cop a nod	take a quick nap
Cop a squat	take your seat
Cut some rug	to dance
I don't give a doodley squat	I couldn't care less
To eyeball someone	to look at someone
Fracture your wig	blow your top
Gams	legs
Gimme some skin	let's shake hands
Grabbers	hands
Grease your chops	to have dinner
Groundpads	feet
Gumbeating	gossiping
In February Hawkins talks	cold and wintry weather
Map	face
Moss	hair
Peepers	eyes
Pitch a boogie-woogie	start a fight
Poppa stoppa	old man
Sky-piece	hat
Slammer	door
Snap a snapper	strike a match
Snap your cap	lose your temper
Stomps	shoes
Struggle-buggy	car
Twister	key
Wig	hair and head
Wooden kimona	coffin

TRADITIONAL AMERICAN

The Turn of the Road

I was playing with my hoop along the road
Just where the bushes are, when, suddenly,
I heard a shout. – I ran away and stowed
Myself beneath a bush, and watched to see
What made the noise, and then, around the bend,
A woman came.

She was old.
She was wrinkle-faced. She had big teeth. – The end
Of her red shawl caught on a bush and rolled
Right off her, and her hair fell down. – Her face
Was white, and awful, and her eyes looked sick,
And she was talking queer.

'*O God of Grace!*'
Said she, '*Where is the child?*' And flew back quick
The way she came, and screamed, and shook her hands!
. . . Maybe she was a witch from foreign lands!

JAMES STEPHENS

Get off this estate

'Get off this estate.'
'What for?'
'Because it's mine.'
'Where did you get it?'
'From my father.'
'Where did he get it?'
'From his father.'
'And where did he get it?'
'He fought for it.'
'Well, I'll fight you for it.'

CARL SANDBURG

Give Me Back My Rags

Just come to my mind
And my thoughts will scratch out your face

Just come into my sight
And my eyes will start snarling at you

Just open your mouth
And my silence will smash your jaws

Just remind me of you
And my remembering will paw up the ground under your feet

That's what it's come to between us

VASKO POPA
Yugoslavian poem translated from the Serbo Croatian by Anne Pennington

In the Orchard

There was a giant by the Orchard Wall
Peeping about on this side and on that,
And feeling in the trees. He was as tall
As the big apple tree, and twice as fat:
His beard poked out, all bristly-black, and there
Were leaves and gorse and heather in his hair.

He held a blackthorn club in his right hand,
And plunged the other into every tree,
Searching for something – You could stand
Beside him and not reach up to his knee,
So big he was – I trembled lest he should
Come trampling, round-eyed, down to where I stood.

I tried to get away. – But, as I slid
Under a bush, he saw me, and he bent
Down deep at me, and said, *'Where is she hid?'*
I pointed over there, and off he went –
But, while he searched, I turned and simply flew
Round by the lilac bushes back to you.

JAMES STEPHENS

The Count Duke of Olivares : Velazquez

This is the sort of face that sheep
Count in the night when they can't sleep.

PAUL ENGLE

Turtle City

Let turtles' patterned shells break the surface of
the shining water
Let them dive to a turtle land beneath the waves, where
are oyster-paved roads and where turtle shells are
instead of houses; turtles plod along the streets.
In dark holes, shrimps and other small creatures lurk.
The brilliant angelfish light the street with yellow glow
Turtles retire to their shells at darkness
And leave the streets to the night fish.

KEVAN HALL

The Tom-Cat

At midnight in the alley
A Tom-cat comes to wail,
And he chants the hate of a million years
As he swings his snaky tail.

tabby Malevolent, bony, brindled,
Tiger and devil and bard,
His eyes are coals from the middle of Hell
And his heart is black and hard.

He twists and crouches and capers
And bares his curved sharp claws,
And he sings to the stars of the jungle nights,
Ere cities were, or laws.

Beast from a world primeval,
He and his leaping clan,
When the blotched red moon leers over the roofs,
Give voice to their scorn of man.

He will lie on a rug tomorrow
And lick his silky fur,
And veil the brute in his yellow eyes
And play he's tame, and purr.

But at midnight in the alley
He will crouch again and wail,
And beat the time for his demon's song,
With the swing of his demon's tail.

DON MARQUIS

The Dreamer

Palmstroem lights a bunch of candles
on the stone plate of his nightstand
and observes it gently melting.

Strangely, now it forms a mountain
out of downward-flowing lava,
models fringes, frostings, spirals.

Quivering above the runlets
stand the wicks with flames uprising
like a golden cypress forest.

On the white romantic rock crags
sees the dreamer's vision flocks of
dauntless sunward-striving pilgrims.

CHRISTIAN MORGENSTERN German poem translated by Max Knight

The World below the Brine

The world below the brine,
Forests at the bottom of the sea, the branches and leaves,
Sea-lettuce, vast lichens, strange flowers and seeds, the thick
    tangle, openings, and pink turf,
Different colours, pale grey and green, purple, white, and gold,
    the play of light through the water,
sticky substance   Dumb swimmers there among the rocks, coral, gluten, grass,
food   rushes, and the aliment of the swimmers,
Sluggish existences grazing there suspended, or slowly crawling
    close to the bottom,
The sperm-whale at the surface blowing air and spray, or
tail fins   disporting with his flukes,
The leaden-eyed shark, the walrus, the turtle, the hairy
    sea-leopard, and the sting-ray,
Passions there, wars, pursuits, tribes, sight in those ocean-
    depths, breathing that thick-breathing air, as so many do,
The change thence to the sight here, and to the subtle air
    breathed by beings like us who walk this sphere,
The change onward from ours to that of beings who walk other
    spheres.

WALT WHITMAN

Thaw in the City

Now my legs begin to walk.
The filthy piles of snow are melting.
Pavements are wet.

What clear, tiny streams!
Suddenly I feel the blood flowing in the veins
in the backs of my hands.

And I hear a voice – a wonderful voice –
as if some one I loved had lifted a window
and called my name.

The streets wash over me like waves.
I sail in the boat of factories and sparrows
out of sight.

LOU LIPSITZ

The New River

Down the river comes a noise!
It is not the voice of rolling waters.
It's only the sounds of man,
Dancing halls and tambourine,
record players/petrol   Phonographs and gasoline,
Human beings gone machine.
Ta-ta-ra-ra boom de-ay.
Killed is the blare of the hunting horn.
The River Gods are gone. Hi!

CHARLES E. IVES

Steel: The Night Shift

platforms   Slung from the gantries cranes
patrol in air and parry
lights the furnaces fling up at them.
Clamour is deepest in the den beneath,
fire fiercest at the frontier where
an arm of water doubles
and disjoints it. There is a principle, a pulse
in all these molten and metallic contraries,
this sweat unseen. For men
facelessly habituated to the glare
outstare it, guide the girders
from their high and iron balconies
and keep the simmering slag-trucks
feeding heap on heap
in regular, successive, sea-on-shore
concussive bursts of dry
and falling sound. And time
is all this measured voice would seem

to ask, until it uncreate
the height and fabric of the light-
lunged, restive, flame-eroded night.

CHARLES TOMLINSON

Psalm of Those who Go Forth before Daylight

The policeman buys shoes slow and careful; the teamster
buys gloves slow and careful; they take care of their feet
and hands; they live on their feet and hands.

The milkman never argues; he works alone and no one speaks
to him; the city is asleep when he is on the job; he puts
a bottle on six hundred porches and calls it a day's work;
he climbs two hundred wooden stairways; two horses are
company for him; he never argues.

The rolling-mill men and sheet-steel men are brothers of
cinders; they empty cinders out of their shoes after the
day's work; they ask their wives to fix burnt holes in the
knees of their trousers; their necks and ears are covered
with a smut; they scour their necks and ears; they are
brothers of cinders.

CARL SANDBURG

Canedolia: an off-concrete scotch fantasia

oa! hoy! awe! ba! mey!

who saw?
rhu saw rum. garve saw smoo. nigg saw tain. lairg saw lagg.
rigg saw eigg. largs saw haggs. tongue saw luss. mull saw yell.
stoer saw strone. drem saw muck. gask saw noss. unst saw cults.
echt saw banff. weem saw wick. trool saw twatt.

how far?
from largo to lunga from joppa to skibo from ratho to shona from
ulva to minto from tinto to tolsta from soutra to marsco from
braco to barra from alva to stobo from fogo to fada from gigha to
gogo from kelso to stroma from hirta to spango.

what is it like there?
och it's freuchie, it's faifley, it's wamphray, it's frandy, it's sliddery.

what do you do?
we foindle and fungle, we bonkle and meigle and maxpoffle. we
scotstarvit, armit, wormit, and even whifflet. we play at cross-stobs,
leuchars, gorbals, and finfan. we scavaig, and there's aye a bit of
tilquhilly. if it's wet, treshnish and mishnish.

what is the best of the country?
blinkbonny! airgold! thundergay!

and the worst?
scrishven, shiskine, scrabster, and snizort.

listen! what's that?
catacol and wauchope, never heed them

tell us about last night
well, we had a wee ferintosh and we lay on the quiraing. it was
pure strontian!

but who was there?
petermoidart and craigenkenneth and cambusputtock and
ecclemuchty and corriehulish and balladolly and altnacanny and
clauchanvrechan and stronachlochan and auchenlachar and
tighnacrankie and tilliebruaich and killieharra and invervannach
and achnatudlem and machrishellach and inchtamurchan and
auchterfechan and kinlochculter and ardnawhallie and
   invershuggle

and what was the toast?
schiehallion! schiehallion! schiehallion!

EDWIN MORGAN

Song of Syllables

ye no wi ci hay
yo wi hay
wi ci hay
yo wi ci no
wi ci ni
   (repeat from start)
wi ni wi ci hay
yo wi hay
wi ci hay
yo wi ci ni hay
yo wi ci ni hay
yo wi how
wi ci hay
yo wi ci no
wi ni no wa.

TRADITIONAL AFRICAN

Southbound on the Freeway

A tourist came in from Orbitville,
parked in the air, and said:

The creatures of this star
are made of metal and glass.

Through the transparent parts
you can see their guts.

Their feet are round and roll
on diagrams – or long

measuring tapes – dark
with white lines.

They have four eyes.
The two in the back are red.

Sometimes you can see a 5-eyed
one, with a red eye turning

on the top of his head.
He must be special –

the others respect him,
and go slow,

when he passes, winding
among them from behind.

They all hiss as they glide,
like inches, down the marked

tapes. Those soft shapes,
shadowy inside

the hard bodies – are they
their guts or their brains?

MAY SWENSON

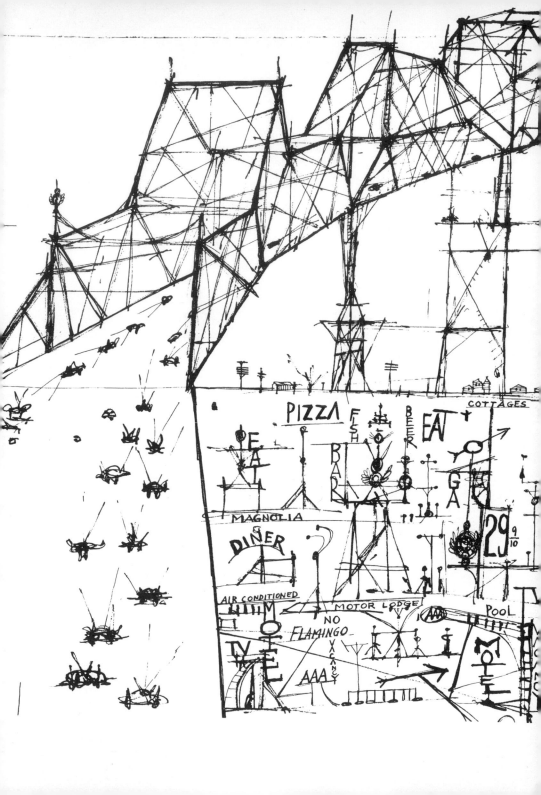

Off Course

the golden flood   the weightless seat
the cabin song   the pitch black
the growing beard   the floating crumb
the shining rendezvous   the orbit wisecrack
the hot spacesuit   the smuggled mouth-organ
the imaginary somersault   the visionary sunrise
the turning continents   the space debris
the golden lifeline   the space walk
the crawling deltas   the camera moon
the pitch velvet   the rough sleep
the crackling headphone   the space silence
the turning earth   the lifeline continents
the cabin sunrise   the hot flood   the space silence
the shining spacesuit   the growing moon
the crackling somersault   the smuggled orbit
the rough moon   the visionary rendezvous
the weightless headphone   the cabin debris
the floating lifeline   the pitch sleep
the crawling camera   the turning silence
the space crumb   the crackling beard
the orbit mouth-organ   the floating song

EDWIN MORGAN

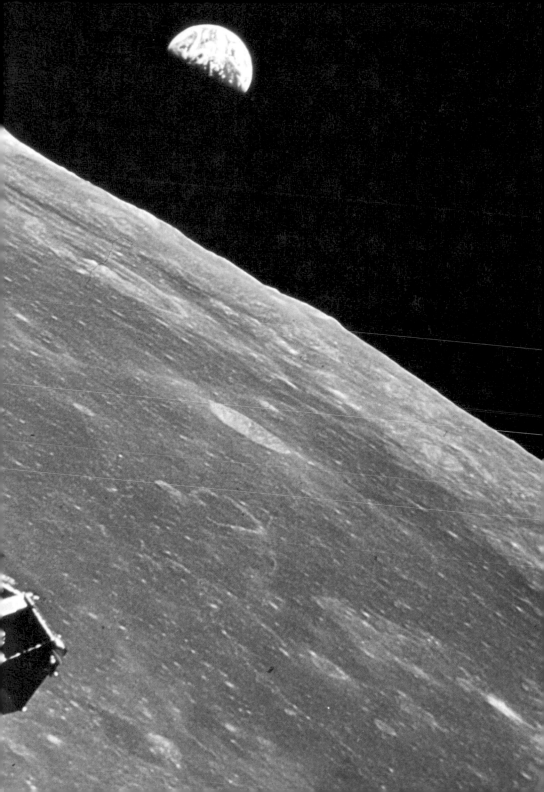

3 Models of the Universe

1   At moment X
the universe began.
It began at point X.
Since then,
through the Hole in a Nozzle,
stars have spewed. An
inexhaustible gush
populates the void forever.

2   The universe was there
before time ran.
A grain
slipped in the glass:
the past began.
The Container
of the Stars expands;
the sand
of matter multiplies forever.

3   From zero radius
to a certain span,
the universe, a Large Lung
specked with stars,
inhales time
until, turgent, it can
hold no more,
and collapses. Then
space breathes, and inhales again,
and breathes again: Forever.

MAY SWENSON

The white man drew a small circle

The white man drew a small circle in the sand
and told the red man, 'This is what the Indian
knows,' and drawing a big circle around the
small one, 'This is what the white man knows.'
The Indian took the stick and swept an immense
ring around both circles: 'This is where the
white man and the red man know nothing.'

CARL SANDBURG

A Prophecy

When pictures look alive with movements free,
When ships, like fishes, swim below the sea,
When men, outstripping birds, can scan the sky,
Then half the world deep drenched in blood shall lie.

ANONYMOUS Written about A.D. 1400

A Dream of Metals

It was then I dreamed
of small metal objects
tacks to secure
casters to run on

I sorted locks, hooks
small nails   bolts and brads
staples loaded in a staple gun

I fill a bureau drawer
with clamps, valves
little wheels, springs
of no known source
or use
which nag to be used

on which I cut myself
and my blood tastes
of copper, silver, and tin

It was then I dreamed
of small metal objects

hinges like cocoons
on the sides of doors
screws thirsty for wood
the hibernation of spikes
on the roadbed

The small metals
trembling as though magnetized

rise one by one
out of the houses they hold together
out of the girders
out of the floorboards
out of the wings of tables

rise up in a cloud / merging
returned to their ore in mid-air
while the cities below them
fall like folded paper

clips, iron filings
the fillings of teeth
sawteeth, tenpenny nails
nuts, pins, and cogs
the strips around the lids of coffee cans

ascending transfigured
like small angels toward the sun

JACK ANDERSON

The Watch

When I
took my
watch to the watchfixer I
felt privileged but also pained to watch the operation. He
had long fingernails and a voluntary squint. He
fixed a magnifying cup over his
squint eye. He
undressed my
watch. I
watched him
split her
in three layers and lay her
innards   middle – a quivering viscera – in a circle on a little plinth. He
shoved shirtsleeves up and leaned like an ogre over my
naked watch. With critical pincers he
poked and stirred. He
lifted out little private things with a magnet too tiny for me
to watch almost. 'Watch out!' I
almost said. His
eye watched, enlarged, the secrets of my
watch, and I
watched anxiously. Because what if he
touched her
ticker too rough, and she
gave up the ghost out of pure fright? Or put her
things back backwards so she'd

run backwards after this? Or he
might lose a minuscule part, connected to her
exquisite heart, and mix her
up, instead of fix her.
And all the time,
all the time-
pieces on the walls, on the shelves, told the time,
told the time
in swishes and ticks,
swishes and ticks,
and seemed to be gloating, as they watched and told. I
felt faint, I
was about to lose my
breath – my
ticker going lickety-split – when watchfixer clipped her
three slices together with a gleam and two flicks of his
tools like chopsticks. He
spat out his
eye, lifted her
high, gave her
a twist, set her
hands right, and laid her
little face, quite as usual, in its place on my
wrist.

MAY SWENSON

Tuba

a flaming tuba
blazes on the boulevard

the flames are wings
and the tuba rises

above the city and up
through the sunlight

a brass kite
sailing to the clouds

harrumping like an uncle
tying his shoelace

who has sprouted wings
that sear through his back

and who finds
he is no longer sitting

by the side of the bed
but flying flying

over bridges and shops
still doubled over

still tightening the laces
while he wheezes and grunts

all along he had known
this would happen

had been waiting
for the day

when he would be flying
waving to the crowds

smiling and nodding
to his astonished friends

but not this way
not bent over

pulling at his shoelace
harrumping harrumping

as he disappears
into the mouth of the sun

MORTON MARCUS

Big Wind

Where were the greenhouses going,
Lunging into the lashing
Wind driving water
So far down the river
_{taps} All the faucets stopped? –
So we drained the manure-machine
For the steam plant,
Pumping the stale mixture
Into the rusty boilers,
Watching the pressure gauge
Waver over to red,
As the seams hissed
And the live steam
Drove to the far
End of the rose-house,
Where the worst wind was,
Creaking the cypress window-frames,
Cracking so much thin glass
We stayed all night,
_{coarse hessian} Stuffing the holes with burlap;
But she rode it out,
That old rose-house,
She hove into the teeth of it,
The core and pith of that ugly storm,
Ploughing with her stiff prow,
Bucking into the wind-waves
That broke over the whole of her,
Flailing her sides with spray,
Flinging long strings of wet across the roof-top,
Finally veering, wearing themselves out, merely
Whistling thinly under the wind-vents;
She sailed until the calm morning,
Carrying her full cargo of roses.

THEODORE ROETHKE

You cannot put a Fire out

You cannot put a Fire out –
A Thing that can ignite
Can go, itself, without a Fan –
Upon the slowest Night –

You cannot fold a Flood –
And put it in a Drawer –
Because the Winds would find it out –
And tell your Cedar Floor –

EMILY DICKINSON

Pyromaniac

In the Coventry Guild accounts
For stage-props and attire
This item stands among the many
That Miracle Plays require:
To Jonathan Williams, fourpence,
For settynge ye Worlde on fyre.

GRAEME WILSON

Wind

This house has been far out at sea all night,
The woods crashing through darkness, the booming hills,
Winds stampeding the fields under the window
Floundering black astride and blinding wet

Till day rose; then under an orange sky
The hills had new places, and wind wielded
Blade-light, luminous black and emerald,
Flexing like the lens of a mad eye.

At noon I scaled along the house-side as far as
The coal-house door. I dared once to look up –
Through the brunt wind that dented the balls of my eyes
The tent of the hills drummed and strained its guyrope,

The fields quivering, the skyline a grimace,
At any second to bang and vanish with a flap:
The wind flung a magpie away and a black-
Back gull bent like an iron bar slowly. The house

Rang like some fine green goblet in the note
That any second would shatter it. Now deep
In chairs, in front of the great fire, we grip
Our hearts and cannot entertain book, thought,

Or each other. We watch the fire blazing,
And feel the roots of the house move, but sit on,
Seeing the window tremble to come in,
Hearing the stones cry out under the horizons.

TED HUGHES

Hide and Seek

Call out. Call loud: 'I'm ready! Come and find me!'
The sacks in the toolshed smell like the seaside.
They'll never find you in this salty dark,
But be careful that your feet aren't sticking out.
Wiser not to risk another shout.
The floor is cold. They'll probably be searching
The bushes near the swing. Whatever happens
You musn't sneeze when they come prowling in.
And here they are, whispering at the door;
You've never heard them sound so hushed before.
Don't breathe. Don't move. Stay dumb. Hide in your blindness.
They're moving closer, someone stumbles, mutters;
Their words and laughter scuffle, and they're gone.
But don't come out just yet; they'll try the lane
And then the greenhouse and back here again.
They must be thinking that you're very clever,
Getting more puzzled as they search all over.
It seems a long time since they went away.
Your legs are stiff, the cold bites through your coat;
The dark damp smell of sand moves in your throat.
It's time to let them know that you're the winner.
Push off the sacks. Uncurl and stretch. That's better!
Out of the shed and call to them: 'I've won!
Here I am! Come and own up I've caught you!'
The darkening garden watches. Nothing stirs.
The bushes hold their breath; the sun is gone.
Yes, here you are. But where are they who sought you?

VERNON SCANNELL

GLASS
WITH CARE

Messrs Matthew Clark & Sons Ltd.,
190, West Ferry Road,
Kilburn,
LONDON, N.11.

PER   CARRIAGE PAID
From RIGBY & EVENS, LTD.,
22, King Street, Queen Square, BRISTOL, 1.

The Forest

Among the primary rocks
where the bird spirits
crack the granite seeds
and the tree statues
with their black arms
threaten the clouds,

suddenly
there comes a rumble,
as if history
were being uprooted,

the grass bristles,
boulders tremble,
the earth's surface cracks

and there grows

a mushroom,

immense as life itself,
filled with billions of cells
immense as life itself,
eternal,
watery,

appearing in this world for the first

and last time.

MIROSLAV HOLUB Czechoslovakian poem translated by George Theiner

The Circus Band

All summer long, we boys
Dreamed 'bout big circus joys!
Down Main Street comes the band, Oh!
'Ain't it a grand and glorious noise!'

    Horses are prancing,
    Knights advancing –
    Helmets gleaming,
    Pennants streaming,
Cleopatra's on her throne!
That gold hair is all her own.

Where is the lady all in pink?
Last year she waved to me I think,
Stop that nonsense! Can she have died? Can that rot!
She is passing but she sees me not.

Where is the clown, that funny gink,
Last year he winked at me I think,
Can he have died? Can that rot!
He's still a-winkin' but he sees me not.

CHARLES E. IVES

Love on the Canal Boat

1   Why is love like a canal boat?
Why is a sword like beer?
When is a man a perfect chimney?
What's the latest thing in boots?

        Watchmakers
        When it's turned round
        It's the sole support of man
        Make the trousers first

2   What is that which works when it plays
    and plays when it works?
Why is there nothing like leather?
Who gets credit for good works?

        It's an internal transport
        An urchin
        A fountain
        It's of no use till it's drawn

3   What's the best way of making a coat last?
When is an egg not oval?
Why is chloroform like Mendelssohn?
What chin is that which is never shaved?

        It's one of the great composers
        When he doesn't smoke
        Stockings

EDWIN J. BRETT

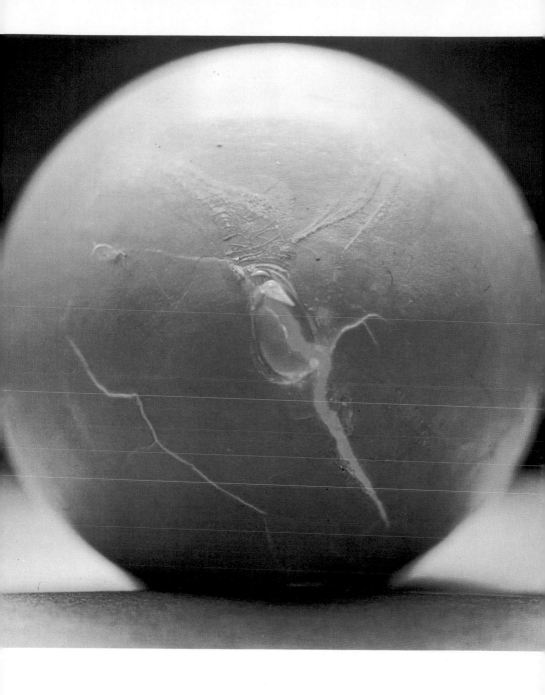

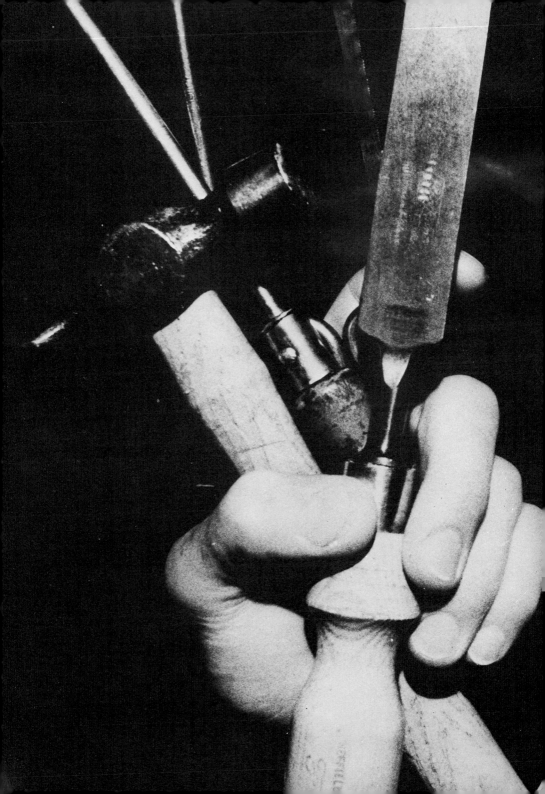

The Nail

One be the nail another the pincers
The others are workmen

The pincers take the nail by the head
With their teeth with their hands they grip him
And tug him tug
To get him out of the ceiling
Usually they only pull his head off
It's difficult to get a nail out of the ceiling

Then the workmen say
The pincers are no good
They smash their jaws they break their arms
And throw them out of the window

After that someone else be the pincers
Someone else the nail
The others are workmen

VASKO POPA
Yugoslavian poem translated from the Serbo Croatian by Anne Pennington

A Boy's Head

In it there is a space-ship
and a project
for doing away with piano lessons.

And there is
Noah's ark,
which shall be first.

And there is
an entirely new bird,
an entirely new hare,
an entirely new bumble-bee.

There is a river
that flows upwards.

There is a multiplication table.

There is anti-matter.

And it just cannot be trimmed.

I believe
that only what cannot be trimmed
is a head.

There is much promise
in the circumstance
that so many people have heads.

MIROSLAV HOLUB Czechoslovakian poem translated by Ian Milner

The Cauliflower

I wanted to be a cauliflower,
all brain and ears,
meditating on the origin of gardens
and the divinity of Him
who carefully binds my leaves.

With my blind roots touched
by the songs of the worms,
and my rough throat throbbing
with strange, vegetable sounds,
perhaps I'd feel the parting stroke
of a butterfly's wing. . . .

Not like my cousins, the cabbages,
whose heads, tightly folded,
see and hear nothing of this world,
dreaming only on the yellow
and green magnificence
that is hardening within them.

JOHN HAINES

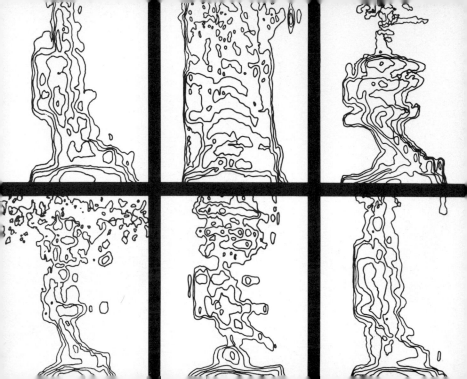

Who do you think you are

Who do you think you are
and where do you think you came from?
From toenails to the hair of your head you are mixed of the earth,
    of the air,
Of compounds equal to the burning gold and amethyst lights
    of the Mountains of the Blood of Christ at Santa Fe.
Listen to the laboratory man tell what you are made of, man,
    listen while he takes you apart.
Weighing 150 pounds you hold 3,500 cubic feet of gas – oxygen,
    hydrogen, nitrogen.
From the 22 pounds and 10 ounces of carbon in you is the filling
    for 9,000 lead pencils.
In your blood are 50 grains of iron and in the rest of your frame
    enough iron to make a spike that would hold your weight.
From your 50 ounces of phosphorus could be made 800,000
    matches and elsewhere in your physical premises are hidden
    60 lumps of sugar, 20 teaspoons of salt, 38 quarts of water, two
    ounces of lime, and scatterings of starch, chloride of potash,
    magnesium, sulphur, hydrochloric acid.
fantastic illusion   You are a walking drug store and also a cosmos and a phantasma-
    goria treading a lonesome valley, one of the people, one of the
    minions and myrmidons who would like an answer to the
    question, 'Who and what are you?'

CARL SANDBURG

Satire

That man came shouting, 'I am a chief.'
Certainly he looks lazy enough for the title;
He also has the appetite of a king's son,
And a very royal waddle.
But he shouts, 'I am a chief':
Therefore I know he is not one.

TRADITIONAL
Gilbert Islands poem translated from a Micronesian language by Arthur Grimble

Transplanting

Watching hands transplanting,
ramming, packing Turning and tamping,
Lifting the young plants with two fingers,
Sifting in a palm-full of fresh loam, –
One swift movement, –
Then plumping in the bunched roots,
A single twist of the thumbs, a tamping and turning,
All in one,
Quick on the wooden bench,
A shaking down, while the stem stays straight,
Once, twice, and a faint third thump, –
Into the flat-box it goes,
Ready for the long days under the sloped glass:

The sun warming the fine loam,
The young horns winding and unwinding,
Creaking their thin spines,
The underleaves, the smallest buds
Breaking into nakedness,
The blossoms extending
Out into the sweet air,
The whole flower extending outward,
Stretching and reaching.

THEODORE ROETHKE

The bed says to the carpenter

The bed says to the carpenter, Do not make me,
For if you do, tomorrow or the day after, they will carry you
    upon me to your grave.
And there will be no one to help you.

The pick says to its proud maker,
Do not make me, for tomorrow or the day after, they will use
    me to dig your grave,
And there will be no one to help you.

The cloth says to the weaver,
Do not weave me, for tomorrow or the day after, I will be your
    shroud.
And there will be no one to help you.

TRADITIONAL Indian poem translated by Shamroo Hivale and Verrier Elwin

Father's Gloves

Not garments. A craftsman's armour
Worn to blunt the hooks of pain.
Massive, white asbestos mitts
He brought back from the shipyard
Hang cool by his blowlamp
And his sailmaker's palm.
In his hearth, treasured still,
Scored by remembered cinders,
Lie gauntlets from his dirt-track days
That sometimes, when his fire is dull,
He wears to prod the embers.
Keeping them rekindles him.

He keeps them all, the pairs
We give him on his birthdays,
Crammed in drawers too full to shut.
Some of them may have a use
At family ceremonial:
But, christening or funeral,
Pigskin, suede, kid or calf,
We'd have him carry them, because
His hands are warmer with them off.

TED WALKER

The Carpenter

With those heavy two
hands of his he'd like
to make a bird, dark-
eyed, delicate, quick-
breathing. But the bones
turn into boxes,
geometry breaks
the heart. So he makes
cages; if a cage
is perfect a bird
lives there.

ERIC TORGERSEN

The penknife glides

The penknife glides through the polystyrene,
turning it to get a good angle.
Smoothly the oiled blade cuts
as my dad carves a goldfish.
All his face is screwed up.
He sees nothing but his moving hand,
and doesn't know I'm there.
Hands last night that were rough, big and clumsy
as the floorboards were torn up,
and thick cable cut to lay beneath.
Now, as I watch,
I wonder at the care of his delicate hands,
As a small perfect goldfish forms.

IAN GRIFFITHS

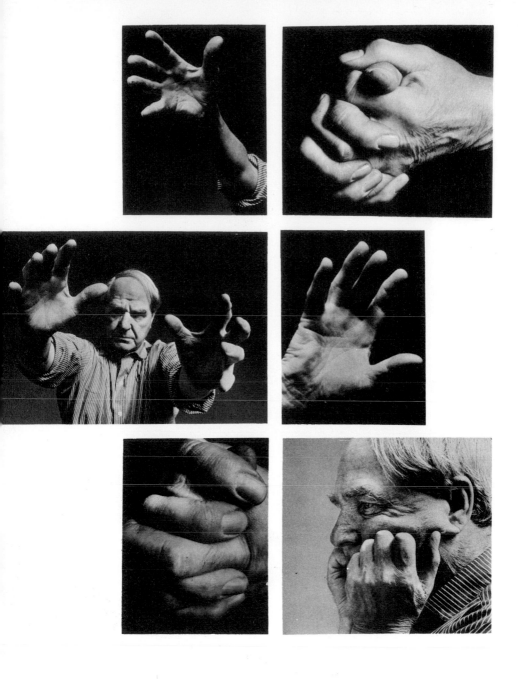

I'm goin' down to the railroad

I'm goin' down to the railroad
Lay my head on the track
But if I see the train a-comin'
I'll jerk it back.

ANONYMOUS

The engingines

The engingines
of the ailingplane
are stuttering
I hope they won't
beginnnn
to stammer:
30,000 feet
is too high for speech defects.

PAUL GOODMAN

Traveller's Choice

imagine Counsel yourself that traveller
Who in a fiery desert found,
When half starved for water,
A well-shaft glimmering in the ground –
No rope nor bucket to be had
And the sweet water twenty foot down –
Should he crouch in the heat and go mad
Or plunge into coolness and drown?

JON STALLWORTHY

Muckers

Twenty men stand watching the muckers.
   Stabbing the sides of the ditch
   Where clay gleams yellow,
   Driving the blades of their shovels
   Deeper and deeper for the new gas mains,
   Wiping sweat off their faces
     With red bandanas.

The muckers work on . . . pausing . . . to pull
Their boots out of suckholes where they slosh.

   Of the twenty looking on
Ten murmur, 'O, it's a hell of a job,'
Ten others, 'Jesus, I wish I had the job.'

CARL SANDBURG

In the Paddy Field

Women, rice-planting:
   all muddy, save for one thing –
     that's their chanting.

RAIZAN Japanese poem translated by Harold G. Henderson

The Collier

When I was born on Amman hill
A dark bird crossed the sun.
Sharp on the floor the shadow fell;
I was the youngest son.

And when I went to the County School
I worked in a shaft of light.
In the wood of the desk I cut my name:
Dai for Dynamite.

The tall black hills my brothers stood;
Their lessons all were done.
From the door of the school when I ran out
They frowned to watch me run.

The slow grey bells they rung a chime
Surly with grief or age.
Clever or clumsy, lad or lout,
All would look for a wage.

I learnt the valley flowers' names
And the rough bark knew my knees.
I brought home trout from the river
And spotted eggs from the trees.

A coloured coat I was given to wear
Where the lights of the rough land shone.
Still jealous of my favour
The tall black hills looked on.

They dipped my coat in the blood of a kid
And they cast me down a pit,
And although I crossed with strangers
There was no way up from it.

Soon as I went from the County School
I worked in a shaft. Said Jim,
'You will get your chain of gold, my lad,
But not for a likely time.'

And one said, 'Jack was not raised up
When the wind blew out the light
Though he interpreted their dreams
And guessed their fears by night.'

And Tom, he shivered his leper's lamp
For the stain that round him grew;
And I heard mouths pray in the after-damp
When the picks would not break through.

They changed words there in darkness
And still through my head they run,
And white on my limbs is the linen sheet
And gold on my neck the sun.

VERNON WATKINS

Steam Shovel

The dinosaurs are not all dead.
I saw one raise its iron head
To watch me walking down the road
Beyond our house today.
Its jaws were dripping with a load
Of earth and grass that it had cropped.
It must have heard me where I stopped,
Snorted white steam my way,
And stretched its long neck out to see,
And chewed, and grinned quite amiably.

CHARLES MALAM

Tottie

As she walked along the street
With her little plates of meat
And the summer sunshine falling on her golden Barnet Fair,
Bright as angels from the skies
Were her dark blue Mutton Pies;
In my East and West Dan Cupid shot a shaft and left it there.

She'd a Grecian I suppose
And of Hampstead Heath two rows,
In her Sunny South they glistened like two pretty strings
    of pearls,
Down upon my bread and cheese
Did I drop and murmur, 'Please
Be my storm and strife, dear Tottie, O, you darlingest of girls.'

Then a bow wow by her side
Who 'til then had stood and tried
A Jenny Lee to banish, which was on his Jonah's Whale,
Gave a hydrophobia bark,
She cried, 'What a Noah's Ark,'
And right through my rank and riches did my cribbage pegs
    assail.

Ere her bull dog I could stop
She had called a ginger pop
Who said, 'What the Henry Meville do you think you're doing
    there?'
And I heard as off I slunk,
'Why the fellow's Jumbo's trunk.'
And the Walter Joyce was Tottie's with the golden
    Barnet Fair. . . .

TRADITIONAL ENGLISH

Rabbit and Pork, Rhyming Talk

Abraham's willing	shilling
All afloat	coat
Barnet Fair	hair
Bread and cheese	knees
Brown Bess	yes
Brown Joe	no
Cain and Abel	table
Cribbage pegs	legs
East and south	mouth
East and west	breast
Eat a fig	'crack a crib'; commit a burglary
Frog and toad	main road
German flutes	pair of boots
Ginger pop	cop
Henry Meville	Devil
Hampstead Heath	teeth
I suppose	nose
Jenny Lee	flea
Jonah's whale	tail
Jumbo's trunk	drunk
Lump of lead	head
Mother and daughter	water
Mutton pies	eyes
Noah's Ark	lark
Plates of meat	feet
Plough the deep	go to sleep
Rank and riches	breeches
Round the houses	trousers
Salmon trout	mouth
Steam-packet	jacket
Storm and strife	wife
Sugar and honey	money
Sunny south	mouth
Take a fright	night
Throw me in the dirt	shirt
Turtle doves	pair of gloves
Two-foot rule	fool
Walter Joyce	voice

TRADITIONAL ENGLISH

Dunce Song

Some day,
When the great clock
Of dawn strikes, and keeps on striking –
What's gone wrong, the president will shout, why doesn't
    somebody,
Somebody stop it? –

That day,
When the music starts
That no man ever heard before –
Bong, bong, the bells up there, whish, whish,
The windy singing –

That time
Will be my time:
No minutes, years, no coming, going –
Night, poor night, laid out in white – oh, my soul,
The death of darkness –

Whee, whee,
The waking birds.
(Yet I do pity them a little –
Come close, I'm whispering – yes, I too will miss their brave
Songs at sunset.)

MARK VAN DOREN

Psalm Concerning the Castle

Let me be at the place of the castle.

Let the castle be within me.

Let it rise foursquare from the moat's ring.

Let the moat's waters reflect green plumage of ducks, let the shells of swimming turtles break the surface or be seen through the rippling depths.

Let horsemen be stationed at the rim of it, and a dog, always alert on the brink of sleep.

Let the space under the first storey be dark, let the water lap the stone posts, and vivid green slime glimmer upon them; let a boat be kept there.

carved pillars Let the caryatids of the second storey be bears upheld on beams that are dragons.

On the parapet of the central room, let there be four archers, looking off to the four horizons. Within, let the prince be at home, let him sit in deep thought, at

galleries, arcades peace, all the windows open to the loggias.

Let the young queen sit above, in the cool air, her child in her arms; let her look with joy at the great circle, the pilgrim shadows, the work of the sun and the play of the wind. Let her walk to and fro. Let the columns uphold the roof, let the storeys uphold the columns, let there be dark space below the lowest floor, let the castle rise foursquare out of the moat, let the moat be a ring and the water deep, let the guardians guard it, let there be wide lands around it, let that country where it stands be within me, let me be where it is.

DENISE LEVERTOV

You can go now

You can go now yes go now. Go east or west, go north or
south, you can go now. Or you can go up or go down now.
And after these there is no place to go. If you say no
to all of them then you stay here. You don't go. You
are fixed and put. And from here if you choose you send
up rockets, you let down buckets. Here then for you is
the centre of things.

CARL SANDBURG

Answers to Riddles

Four Natural Songs (Riddles) page 19

1 Birds   2 Sun   3 Grass   4 Clouds

Love on the Canal Boat page 76

The questions and answers are in no particular order in this poem. You could arrange everything the way you prefer.

Tunes for Some Poems

The Hob-Nailed Boots what Farver Wore

My far-ver's feet filled up arf a street So his boots were in pro-

por-tion, And the kids he'd squash in a week, by gosh! It

really was a cau-tion. Well, me and me bruvvers at the

age of four, All wrapped up cosy in a box of straw, Till el-

ev-en in the mor-ning used to sleep and snore, In the

hob-nailed boots what far-ver wore.

The Death of Ned Kelly

Ned Kel-ly fought the rich men in coun-try and in town, Ned

Kel-ly fought the troo-pers un-til they ran him down; He

thought that he had fooled them, for he was hard to find, But he

rode in-to Glen-row-an with the troo-pers close be-hind.

Go Down, Moses

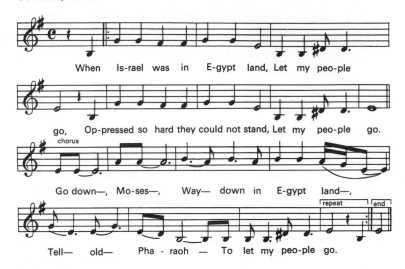

When Is-rael was in E-gypt land, Let my peo-ple

go, Op-pressed so hard they could not stand, Let my peo-ple go.

chorus

Go down—, Mo-ses—, Way— down in E-gypt land—,

repeat   end

Tell— old— Pha-raoh — To let my peo-ple go.

Pretty Boy Floyd

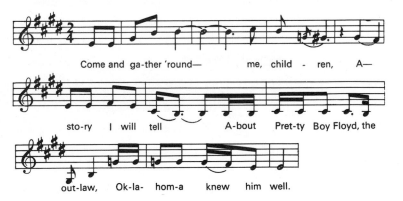

Come and ga-ther 'round— me, child - ren, A—

sto-ry I will tell A-bout Pret-ty Boy Floyd, the

out-law, Ok-la- hom-a knew him well.

Whisky in the Jar

As I was go-ing o-ver Gil- gar-ra Mount-ain, I

met Colo-nel Pep-per and his mo-ney he was count-ing. I

drew forth my pis-tols and I rat- tled my sa-bre Say-ing

chorus

'Stand and de- liv-er, for I am a bold de- cei-ver'. Mush-a

ring-um dur-am da, Whack! fol de dad- dy- o,

Whack! fol de dad- dy- o, There's whis-ky in the jar.

Tottie

As she walked a- long the street With her lit- tle plates of meat And the

su- mmer sun- shine fall- ing on her gol- den Bar – net Fair, Bright as

an- gels from the skies Were her dark blue Mutt- on Pies; In my

East and West Dan Cup- id shot a shaft and left it there.

Acknowledgements

For permission to use copyright material acknowledgement is made to the following:

Poetry For 'A Dream of Metals' by Jack Anderson from *31 New American Poets* to the author; for 'Roman Wall Blues' from *Collected Shorter Poems* by W. H. Auden to Faber & Faber Ltd and Random House Inc.; for 'Beauty' and 'Clouds' by Matsuo Bashō from *An Introduction to Haiku* edited by Harold G. Henderson to Doubleday & Co. Inc.; for 'Love on the Canal Boat' by Edwin J. Brett from *Pioneers of Modern Poetry* to the author and Kayak; for 'Had they no voice' by Chiyo from *An Introduction to Haiku* edited by Harold G. Henderson to Doubleday & Co. Inc.; for 'Knock, knock, who's there?' from *Knock Knock* by Bob Dunn to the Western Publishing Co. Inc.; for 'The Engingines' from *Hawkweed* by Paul Goodman to Random House Inc.; for 'The Wreckers' Prayer' by Theodore Goodridge Roberts to the author; for 'The penknife glides' by Ian Griffiths to the author; for 'The Cauliflower' by John Haines from *31 New American Poets* to the author; for 'Turtle City' by Kevan Hall to the author and *Living Language*, BBC Schools Radio; for 'A Boy's Head', 'The Door', 'A Dog in the Quarry' and 'The Forest' from *Selected Poems* by Miroslav Holub translated by Ian Milner to Penguin Books Ltd; for 'Wind' from *Hawk in the Rain* by Ted Hughes to Faber & Faber Ltd and Harper & Row Inc.; for 'The Circus Band' and 'The New River' by Charles E. Ives to the author; for 'A Pict Song' from *Puck of Pook's Hill* by Rudyard Kipling to Mrs George Bambridge, Macmillan & Co. Ltd and Doubleday & Co. Inc.; for 'Psalm Concerning the Castle' from *Sorrow Dance* by Denise Levertov to Jonathan Cape Ltd and New Directions Publishing Corporation; for 'Thaw in the City' from *Cold Water* by Lou Lipsitz to the Wesleyan University Press; for 'Interruption to a Journey', 'King of Beasts' and 'An Ordinary Day' from *Surroundings* by Norman MacCaig to the Hogarth Press Ltd; for 'Steam Shovel' from *Upper Pasture* by Charles Malem to Holt, Rinehart & Winston Inc.; for 'Tuba' from *Origins* by Morton Marcus to the author and Kayak; for 'The Tom-Cat' by Don Marquis to Doubleday & Co. Inc.; for 'Canedolia: an off-concrete scotch fantasia' and 'The Starlings in George Square' from *The Second Life* by Edwin Morgan to Edinburgh University Press; for 'Off Course' by Edwin Morgan to the author; for 'The Dreamer' and 'The Names of the Months' from *Gallows Songs* by Christian Morgenstern translated by Max Knight to the University of California Press; for 'Give me back my rags' and 'The Nail' from *Selected Poems* by Vasko Popa translated by Anne Pennington to Penguin Books Ltd; for 'In the Paddy Field' by Raizan from *An Introduction to Haiku* edited by Harold G. Henderson to Doubleday & Co. Inc.; for 'Odds and Ends' from *Ounce, Dice, Trice* by Alastair Reid to J. M. Dent & Sons Ltd and Atlantic-Little, Brown & Co.; for 'The Barber Shop' and 'This subway station' from *By the Waters of Manhatten* by Charles Reznikoff to New Directions Publishing Corporation; for 'Big Wind', 'The Meadow Mouse', 'On the Quay' and 'Transplanting' from *Collected Poems* by Theodore Roethke to Faber & Faber Ltd and Doubleday & Co. Inc.; for 'Get off this estate', 'The man put green spectacles on his cow', 'The white man drew a small circle', 'Who do you think you are' and 'You can go now' from *The People, Yes* by Carl Sandburg to Harcourt, Brace & World Inc.; for 'Muckers' from *Chicago Poems* and 'Psalm of Those who Go Forth before Daylight' from *Cornhuskers* by Carl Sandburg to Holt,

Rinehart & Winston Inc.; for 'Hide and Seek' from *Walking Wounded* by Vernon Scannell to Eyre & Spottiswoode Ltd; for 'Traveller's Choice' from *Out of Bounds* by Jon Stallworthy to the Oxford University Press; for 'In the Orchard' and 'The Turn of the Road' from *Collected Poems* by James Stephens to Macmillan & Co. Ltd, the Macmillan Company of Canada and the Macmillan Company of New York; for 'Four Natural Songs (Riddles)', 'Southbound on the Freeway', '3 Models of the Universe' and 'A Yellow Circle' from *To Mix with Time* and 'The Watch' from *Half Sun Half Sleep* by May Swenson to Charles Scribner's Sons; for 'dog in the street', 'stretched out' and 'unforgettable' from *Poems to Eat* by Ishikawa Takuboku translated by Carl Sesar to Kodensha International; for 'Steel: The Night Shift' from *A Peopled Landscape* by Charles Tomlinson to the Oxford University Press; for 'The Carpenter' by Eric Torgensen from *Intro No. 1* edited by R. V. Cassill to Bantam Books Inc.; for 'Dunce Song' and 'Morning Worship' from *New and Collected Poems 1924–1963* by Mark van Doren to Hill & Wang Inc.; for 'Father's Gloves' from *The Solitaries* by Ted Walker to Jonathan Cape Ltd and George Braziller Inc.; for 'The Collier' from *The Ballad of Mari Lwyd and Other Poems* by Vernon Watkins to Faber & Faber Ltd; for 'Pyromaniac' by Graeme Wilson to the author and the *Spectator*; for 'The Wild Geese Leave' by Yasui from *An Introduction to Haiku* edited by Harold G. Henderson to Doubleday & Co. Inc.

Pictures For the picture facing page 1 to Jerry Uelsmann; page 5 from *The World of Camera*, photo Oswald Kettenberger, to C. J. Bucher Ltd; page 9 to Magnum Photos; pages 11, 62–3, 78, 81 to Keith Morris; page 14 to Brassai; page 18 to PAF International Ltd; pages 21, 73 to the Tate Gallery, London; pages 24–6 from *Ounce, Dice, Trice* by Alastair Reid to Atlantic-Little, Brown & Co.; pages 29, 93 to John Brooke; page 31 to SPADEM, Paris; page 33 to Sidney Nolan and the Marlborough Gallery, London; page 34 from *The Oxford Illustrated Old Testament* Volume 1 to Oxford University Press; page 40 to A. V. Allmen; pages 42–3 to John Walmsley; page 45 to the Museo del Prado, Madrid; pages 48, 98 and title-page to the Trustees of the British Museum; pages 54–5 from *The Labyrinth* by Saul Steinberg to the artist and Hamish Hamilton Ltd; pages 56–7 to Keystone Press Agency Ltd; pages 64, 68 to Geoffrey Drury; page 67 to Harry Callahan; page 71 to Rex Features Ltd; page 74 to the Hampshire County Museum; page 77 to Jiří Macák; page 87 to John Hedgecoe; page 88 to the Musée de l'Air, Paris; page 91 to the George Eastman Collection, New York.

Every effort has been made to trace owners of copyright material, but in some cases this has not proved possible. The publishers would be glad to hear from any further copyright owners of material reproduced in *Junior Voices*.

List of Illustrations

Index of Titles and First Lines

Index of Poets, Translators and Collectors